THE SPIRIT OF
TIDESWELL
THE 20TH CENTURY IN PHOTOGRAPHS

Tony Hill and Paul Black

THE SPIRIT OF
TIDESWELL

THE 20TH CENTURY IN PHOTOGRAPHS

Tony Hill and Paul Black

Published by

Landmark Publishing Ltd,

Ashbourne Hall, Cokayne Ave, Ashbourne, Derbyshire DE6 1EJ England
Tel: (01335) 347349 Fax: (01335) 347303
e-mail: landmark@clara.net www.landmark publishing.co.uk

1st edition

ISBN 1 84306-010-8

Print: MPG Ltd, Bodmin, Cornwall
Design: Mark Titterton
Cover by James Allsopp

Front cover: The Three Tuns Inn.

Front cover: The charabanc photograph depicts members of the church choir trip
to Blackpool in August 1925.

Back cover Middle: Tideswell Majorettes 1959.

Back cover Bottom: The King's Head (demolished 1958) stood to the right, as one exited the main
gates of the church yard.

Title page: An early photograph of the Fountain.

Contents

I was born and bred in Tidza and proud of it. I have seen many changes in the village having been born in 1942. In fact we have traced the family back to the 1600s in Tideswell, so I can truly say I am local.

I have many childhood memories of Tideswell: The gasworks where I watched Ernest Locke, Tom Smith, Frank Watkins and Gilley Peach, feed the retorts and drag the hot coke from them; the steam powered beer lorry delivering barrels of beer to the Kings Head; going to see the pictures in the evenings, sometimes three times in one week, with queues often down past Blake House; a visit to see Dr. Brookes at his surgery in Eccles Hall and watching him mowing his lawn from the examination room window, hoping he would remember he had sent me in there three hours before; I remember the village having two local bobbies. Woe betide you if you were caught riding two on a bike, there was no vandalism in those days; Mac Bothamley, the Town Crier, ringing his bell and shouting out his messages; Jim Walton and Harold Walker, the local farmers, delivering their milk in bulk on the handlebars of their bicycles and ladling it out into the customer's large milk jugs. Then there were the night watchmen, whenever any road works were being carried out, sitting in a little cabin with their hot smoking brazier burning outside the doorway on cold winter nights; the Sunday School pantomime; the swings in the playground which were chained and locked every Sunday; whist drives, beetle drives, and attending youth club at the Congregational Church; visiting Joe's Café on a Saturday night after the pubs closed or drinking tea and coffee and playing cards in Libby's Café, (which was decorated with wallpaper that had cost her ten and six a roll) situated where the Madeira House Restaurant is today.

All my nostalgic memories. But these are only memories that will die with me. The photographic image never dies; it is the factual record of a moment in history.

I became interested in collecting old photographs of the village for the above reason and started collecting them more seriously when I retired four years ago. I have had small exhibitions of them during Wakes Week; Paul also had a large selection of postcards of Tideswell. Between us, we agreed we had enough material for a book. Lindsey Porter of Landmark Publishing gave us the final nudge and here is the result.

What Paul and myself have tried to achieve with this book is to provide a general record of changes, people, achievements, and events in Tideswell and its surrounding villages in the twentieth century. We hope to jog the memories of some people, and inform others, of what Tideswell and some outlying villages were like in the last century. It is not intended to be a comprehensive record of the area. It just happens to consist of photographs we have in our possession at the time of going to print.

Please, if you have any more photographs of Tideswell and its locality, we would be very interested to see them and scan them. Who knows, if there is sufficient interest, a second volume could be the result. Contact me at Hills 'n' Dales, Queen Street, Tideswell.

Many thanks to my father, Archie Hill, who has been our constant source of information.

Finally, last but not least, special thanks to my long suffering wife, June, for her patience over the last few months while Paul and myself have sorted through the photographs, leaving them scattered, for days at a time, over every level surface in the house.

Tony Hill

I first came to Tideswell in 1977. I had been invited to attend an interview for a teaching post at Bishop Pursglove School, the village primary school. I had never visited the Peak District, let alone Tideswell, prior to this. On getting out of the car I was struck, immediately, by the smell of coal smoke in the air. Looking around, I noticed smoke issuing from a number of chimneys and this was a summer evening in June! The harsh and changeable climate has impacted, in my opinion, on the character of the village and its people.

"What a lovely day!" local people will observe, when overhead the sky is grey and threatening. They really mean that it is not actually raining, a situation that is quite rare in Tideswell.

Over the years I have developed a keen interest in the village, its traditions and history. However, I lack the insight available to a 'native' of Tideswell. Personally, I try to take care to avoid wild and scurrilous accusations aimed at long established Tideswell residents, knowing that for some of my friends, who are native to the village, those criticized are likely to be near or distant relatives.

During the development of this volume, Tony's local knowledge has been valuable in that we may have been able to minimize errors in information presented, by resorting to his personal recollections and personal connections (either with those illustrated in photographs or with those individuals who have knowledge of the background of information relating to photographs reproduced).

We are both aware that although we have tried to avoid textual errors, there are many grey areas in terms of our knowledge and also aspects of the pictorial record for which we do not have hard explanatory evidence. For errors we apologize and for the gaps in the information, we would seek help from anyone who can advise us of the correct interpretation of the material we have been able to obtain.

We hope that at the very least we have provided a source of information which will prove entertaining and informative and that, in a small measure we may have fostered an awareness of the vibrancy and spirit of the inhabitants of this part of England.

I dedicate my part of this work to Kathryn, my wife, and to Sandra Mary Elder (1945-2000), my sister.

Paul Black

Acknowledgements

We could not have put this book together without the considerable generosity and help we have received from the many people who took the time and trouble to lone us their photographs for copying. Sincere apologies to anyone we have missed out.

Thanks to: -

Dennis Allsopp; Sally and Paul Andrew; Mary Ayers; Harry Ball; Margaret Bagshaw; Vera Bothamley; Reg Bingham; Mary Bingham; Brenda Bowyer; Dorothy Bradwell; Camille Bricka; Keith Burns; Audrey and Derek Buckley; Peter Cartledge; Jason Chadwick (the photographer of the Buxton Advertiser); Lillian Chapman; Alison Chapman; Douglas Chapman; Elaine Chapman; Peter Cheetham; Howard Crowe; Catherine Dalton; Hazel and Clive Fell; Pat and Duncan Fletcher; Bryan George; Hazel and Derek Gibson; Nellie Gibson; Maude Gratton; Denise Hadjipetrou; Gordon Hallam; David Hall; Irene Hall; Eric Heaf; Lynn Ford; Sylvia and Neville Frost; Anne Hallows; Graham Haslam; Eric Heaf; Barbara and Peter Hicks; Dianne Holbrook; Sara Hollis; Audrey and Brian Hopkins; Ann Hunstone; Freda Kenworthy; Mary and Barry Landen; Mrs. Lewis; Connie Making; Ray Manley (Peak Park Planning Board Photographer); Alan McGuiness; Eddie Megson; Sonia and Julian Motley; Judith and Paul Mount; Pete Nash; Freda and Wilfred Oven; Elsie Repton; Verna Richmond; Rita Robinson; Jean and Joyce Robinson; Len and Dorothy Sellars; Betty and Derek Skidmore; Angela Taylor; Irene and David Taylor; Tish and Ken Tetsill; Denvil Tibbles; Kathleen Turner; Florence Turner; Bob Walkden; Susan and Richard Walker; Robert Walker; Brenda Willis; Muriel Wilshaw; Jenny Whitehouse; Brian Woodhall; Sheila and Allan Yarranton.

Records of Tideswell extend back to ancient times and we know that the environs of the village have evolved in significant ways from these records. However, a perusal of the following photographs reveal the reality of the pace of change since this medium was used for producing a pictorial record of the village.

To many visitors the church is synonymous with the touristic and/or religious image of the village. Churches and chapels are dealt with elsewhere in the volume. However, we begin with a brief look at the area in and around the church building.

The Xmas Greeting picture from 1935 does indicate, on close examination, the congested state of the churchyard gravestones. Later, in the 1950s the road to the south of the church was widened and the churchyard rearranged and rationalized.

Bells awaiting hanging 1929 (increasing the peal from five to eight).

This atmospheric view of the north side of the churchyard shows, again, the congestion of the gravestones prior to the reorganization of this area.

The photograph of the DeBower tomb shows the way in which the pews have been reorganized in the Lytton chapel.

This view of the Pot Market shows the way in which this area was opened up after the demolition of the King's Head.

A general view showing the positioning of the former King's Head Hotel relative to the Church.

Above: The view of the King's Head Hotel, which was demolished in 1957, gives an indication of the size of this hostelry. Note the narrow road, which leads into the Pot Market and the petrol pump to the left of the front door.

Left: The associated picture is, in our opinion, a remarkable image. It shows an unknown group inside the King's Head Hotel. They were out on a circular walk on Easter Sunday 1940. Note the 'Black Out' notice on the wall behind the group. These people were photographed in Wheston and Dam Dale on the same day.

Above: The cottage on the left is reputed to be the original Tideswell Grammar School, which was founded by Bishop Pursglove in 1560. The first floor was the accommodation for the master.

Left: This photograph of St. John's Institute dates from around 1905. It shows the fencing, now removed, which was to be found in this part of the churchyard.

Above: The Old Vicarage was under construction in Parson Brown's time, the late 1700s and early 1800s, having replaced the former Vicarage where the George Hotel now stands. The current Vicarage is located on Pursglove Drive. **Below:** This photograph shows the Old Grammar School along with the old and current village school (on the hillside behind). To the east of the Old Grammar School stands St. John's Institute which faces over the Potter's Field, an area where the poor were buried (in the northern shadow of the church) in former times.

Swinging to the East we have an excellent view of the church roof with its architectural or constructional 'mistake' exhibited in the change of roof levels between nave and chancel. In the background we can see the 'new' George Hotel, the premises of Courtyard Kitchens and Bathrooms and in the further distance the Ex-Servicemen's Club, located on the former site of The Cross Daggers Inn.

Turning to the South the panorama is of Commercial Road. This was formally named The Shambles. In those days the road extended in width only as far as the white line in the middle of the road.

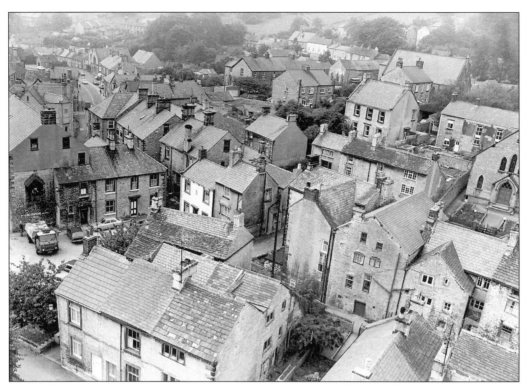

Turning to the west we see the tangle of streets that formed the medieval open market. The Market Charter was granted in 1215, and one can imagine the scene on Market days throughout the centuries. Somewhere in this vista, would have stood Ashe Hall, now disappeared.

The field to the rear right of the final panoramic photograph, in this scene, is known as Alleys Field, a curious name, for which these authors would like some etymological explanation.

This photograph shows the area now known as Bank Corner. By 1904 the Old Guildhall had clearly reached a fairly advanced stage of dilapidation, which led, ultimately, to its demolition and the reuse of the site.

This photograph shows the bank site nearing completion. The present day Post Office, in Church Street, can be seen in the background.

This early photograph of the Guildhall shows, again, the poor state into which the structure had fallen. The building to the right was the old bank, which had various commercial uses throughout the century and in 2000 was converted to the Corner Chippie.

This view of Queen Street shows the bank building, which replaced the Guildhall. We also have an excellent view of the former A.F. Hancock's shops. The shop window on the left of the premises was part of the general grocery store and on the right was the chemist shop. The building to the right of Hancock's is Hunter's general grocers' store, which was demolished in the 1960s and is now Bank Square Gardens.

The panoramic view of Fountain Square also gives an impression of the size of the Velvet Mill up Summer Cross. It also shows vacant open sites, which have now been developed.

Here are two views looking down Church Street with the County Bank on the right.

These scenes of the Fountain predate the war memorial, which was built 1922. Three of the four original corner stumps form part of the new fountain scheme which was completed in the year 2000.

An excellent view of the Fountain in its heyday.

This remarkable picture must be the final image taken of the sandstone structure known as the Fountain. Here it is in the process of demolition in 1935. The present public toilets replaced it. Note the telephone box, which was in the same position as it is today. Most of the dressed stone was broken up and used as hardcore in the base of the toilets. The gritstone stumps were set aside and later used for the base of the see-saws in the play-grounds at Whitecross Road, Pinfold Estate and Town Head.

The War Memorial, which was built in 1922.

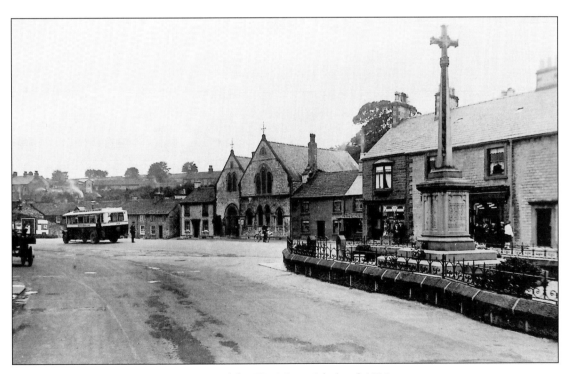

A view of the War Memorial, dated 1934.

A fascinating photograph of the wares in the window of the shop in Fountain Street, which changed ownership many times during the twentieth century, it eventually became Ron Hall's butchers.

Across the road from the Fountain, where the current Hills'n'Dales Tea Room now stands, we have views of the former workshop occupied by the Lomas Brothers, who were builders and joiners until the early 1920s. They were then followed by the Chapman family of joiners and undertakers.

Looking in a southerly direction down Buxton Road, we have a view of Tideswell Brook before it was culverted.

The view looking up Buxton Road shows how little this area has changed over the last eighty to one hundred years.

Town End clustered around the lower end of Buxton Road. In the middle distance to the right of centre of this view we can see the former Tithe Barn before Pinfold Estate was built.

The photograph dating from 1905 shows work in progress in confining Tideswell Brook within a culvert (behind the girls).

This was a New Year's greeting card featuring 'Tondu', known locally as the Clock House, on the edge of the village.

Although not strictly within Tideswell, the Plantation Houses stood where the Picnic Area (in Tideswell Dale) is now situated.

The rather wet view of High Street shows a number of commercial properties. The front elevation of Willis Burns Ltd. now has a much more modern appearance, while the establishments on the left have since changed their use. The premises in front of the gentleman looking towards the camera were Barber's Chip Shop, and the property behind him was Bradbury's grocery and sweet shop.

This is a view looking up High Street shows up a number of changes which have taken place in the area. Note the buildings on each side of The Star Inn.

A march in High Street with Tideswell Band in attendance. The banner says "Royal Mysterious Lodge of the Peak". This, as far as can be ascertained, is a sick club of which there were quite a number in Tideswell. Most families in the village subscribed to one of them before the N.H.S. was created.

A gathering in Market Square.

Tideswell Cattle Fair in September 1907.

A Wakes Fair possibly in the 1930s.

The posed photograph, taken in the Market Square, shows a scene that is clearly recognizable today. The building, directly behind the two male figures, is the former Three Tuns Public House. The road leading off to the right is known as Hollow Gate and was a former route from the village into the Royal Forest of the Peak.

Eccles Hall

This view of pupils outside Eccles Hall is not dated, but as they are all girls and the Grammar School was for boys, the picture is a bit of a mystery!

As we move towards the Market Square we pass Eccles Hall on our right. Samuel Eccles, who was a member of the legal profession, erected this building in the 18th century. The Governors of the Pursglove Trust later purchased it for the Tideswell Grammar School, as a residence for the headmaster, and boarding accommodation for the pupils. When the school was closed in 1930 it was sold to Dr. Brookes for his surgery and private dwelling house.

A view inside Eccles Hall showing the Oak Room used as a dining room for Tideswell Grammar School.

Bagshaw Hall is a fine limestone building built in 1872 in the Italian Style and situated in the Market Square. John Bagshaw financed it at a total cost of £2000 including the clock. Most locals know it as the Picture House. This was closed in the 1970s and was regularly used for public meetings and dances. Note the horse trough.

A copy of one of the dance tickets from June 1964.

These two views are of The Shed, Manchester Road. The former Weaving Shed wove calico and cotton cloth for shirts until the Second World War. Swift Levick's Ltd., of Sheffield then bought it for the manufacture of magnets. These pictures were taken in the early 1970s shortly before it closed. The top one, taken from what is now Holdsworth's car parking area indicates the formidable size of the buildings. Note the north light roof of the foundry and workshops. The lower picture is taken inside the foundry itself and shows the stacks of moulds and the furnace for the castings. Note how much light is directed inside the building from the north light roof. The premises now house Holdswoth's Frozen Food Centre.

Above left: In ancient times stone crosses were erected on all the roads leading into the village. Only the hollowed out bases still remain. These became known as wishing wells. Children used to place crossed straws into them, and make their wish. Butterton Cross is now built into the wall and is situated at the end of Sherwood Road, on the way to Meadow Farm, by the old road to Millers Dale, at the spot where the last glimpse of Tideswell Church can be seen. **Above right:** This example is situated on the right hand side of the road leading into Wheston, about 100 yards past Cross Gates Farm.

Sherwood Road

We have very few good images of Sherwood Road (formerly Back Lane). This picture is a fairly early one and shows the area near the edge of the village. Since this date a great deal of building restoration has been carried out. The top of Brockley Lane is just behind the telegraph pole.

This view shows the area of Sherwood Road around the top of Sunny Bank Lane with an excellent panorama over the village.

The third photograph from Sherwood Road shows Hardy House, which is located at the top of Hardy Lane. At the time this photograph was taken the Newton family occupied the house. The greenhouse was demolished some years ago, although, externally, the house remains substantially the same.

This photograph shows a view of Statuary House on Alma Road. Note the boot scraper on the wall facing the road. This apparatus must have been very useful in the days of horse transport if you were not careful where you put your feet. The reader may be interested when perambulating around Tideswell to see how many of these scrapers still exist.

A view looking down Terrace Road with the church in the background.

These two views of Town Head are taken from Wheston Bank. Although both photographs have a real period 'feel' to them the view is almost identical today, and would be easily recognized by the characters pictured.

Above: This excellent view of Craven House and Town Head gives further evidence of the slow rate of change in this area.

COME AND DRINK IN THE BEAUTIES OF TIDESWELL

Don't you wish that you were me,
Carrying home the X's three.

Left: Tideswell was becoming a tourist destination in the early part of the century. This card is postmarked 1912.

John Lomas after making and fixing new doors for the south porch, 1905.

Canon Samuel Andrew, Vicar of Tideswell 1864-1900, looking at a piece of carving by Advent Hunstone.

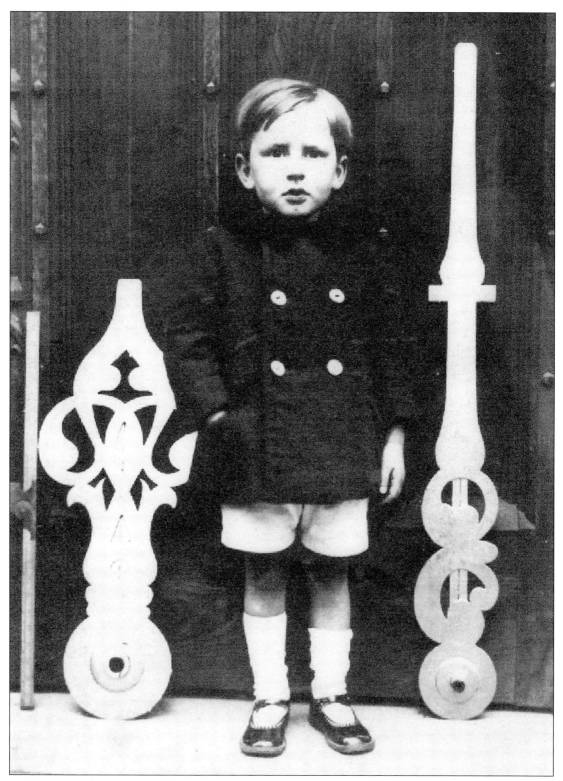

This young chap is Lester Chapman. He is standing between the hands of the church clock outside the doors of Tideswell Church. Date around 1920.

Mrs Robert Brightmore, with her pet bird in the cage, sitting in her garden at Sherwood House, Sherwood Road, at the beginning of the century.

Emma and George Walton who owned and ran a small grocery and toffee shop which was situated on the corner of Cherry Tree Square. It was known to the locals as Emma's. It was closed in the 1960s and has been converted into a dwelling house called The Old Toffee Shop.

Mrs Bingham standing on the doorstep of her Manchester Road cottage built in 1862. Note the initials R L on the keystone over the door– standing for Reuben Leach.

Johnnie Allsop, posing with his small truck in front of the school on St. Johns Road in the 1930s. He used to run a greengrocer's shop and a taxi service from the premises where the Launderette is now situated.

Jack (Snowy) Cartledge was a quarry worker. It was a necessary duty to eliminate foxes to protect the livestock of the many smallholdings in the area.

Below: Joe Sellars the local blacksmith & farrier. He followed his father, Leonard, into the business. His elder brother, Arthur, would have taken it over but he was killed in the First World War.

Above: Sam Millington in the 1930s, outside his cottage opposite the Horse and Jockey. He was a wheelbarrow farmer and employed as a dustman emptying the bins for the Parish Council.

Left: This is Stanley Barber holding a Russian Red Star. A Russian P.O.W took it off his hat and gave it to Stanley during the liberation of Guernsey. The picture was taken for the *Buxton Advertiser* on the fiftieth anniversary of the liberation.

Don Gibson, one of the drivers for Bull's Coaches. He was well known for driving the station bus to Millers Dale.

Harold Andrew the founder of the Andrew's Coaches. Here he is in 1946 in front of The Anchor Inn with both of his coaches. The company began around 1932 when Harold had a taxi business, at the Anchor Garage, which, at that time, was an all-wood building. He then expanded and added a bus to the business. The bus was very successful and others were added. Brian, his son, came into the business in the mid fifties, and took over when Harold died in 1964. In the 1970s Brian's sons, Robert and Paul joined the business, and their sons Russell and Matthew are now involved. Four generations of the Andrew family! Harold has certainly left his mark.

Jim Morris and his wife Eva in Jim's barber's shop. Jim had a very distinguished war record, serving in the 1st Army in Africa. He received the 1939 –45 Star, The Africa Star, the Defence Medal and the George Medal. He was also a very high rank in the St John's Ambulance Brigade, was Director of Ceremonies for Tideswell Band for a number of years and a member of Tideswell Male Voice Choir.

He was known locally as 'Two Minute Jim'. He traded from the early 1950s to the early 1970s when he semi-retired to the house next to the Launderette. He converted a small outbuilding there, which was entered from Church Street, and continued trading for another few years until ill health caused his retirement.

This picture came from the collection of the Lomas family who were well-known joiners and builders at the beginning of the 20th century. Written on the back of the photo was 'Sparger in the cart'. The dandy fellow talking to him appears to be an interesting character also.

Left: Charlie Gregory a local farm labourer and stone waller.

From left to right; Ron Hall, the butcher trading in Fountain Street, and Trevor Hall who used to be the Tideswell Postman for many years. We don't know the character in the middle!

Left: Joseph Richard Slack, a local builder and bandsman, with Bill Watson.

Below: Bill Lawrence, Tideswell Bandmaster, who worked at I.C.I., with Bill Watson and 'friend'.

Norman Gregory, who owned a small grocer's shop on Lower Terrace Road, with John Hall.

Percy Hattersley, a railwayman, and Bill Jackson who worked in the I.C.I. offices.

Arnold Walker, a local farmer, with an admirer.

Arnold Cartledge, a dry stone waller, and Eric Walton a local farmer.

Above: Jim Cooper, a quarryman, Dick Lomas a plasterer, and George Page who worked as a stone-mason for the railway.

Left: Dr. Brookes, came to Tideswell around 1931 and lived at Osbourne House on Buxton Road. He came as an assistant to Dr. Quarnborough who was based at Foxlow House. Eventually, he took over the practice and moved into Foxlow House. During the war years Dr. Brookes ran the practice himself with a lot of assistance from his wife Grace. He eventually moved from Foxlow House to Eccles Hall where he remained until his death, at the age of 72, in 1975.

Maurice Markovitz was born in Plock, Poland, in 1887 and came to Manchester as a refugee. He had one brother, Max, who was killed in the Great War, and four sisters. The family moved to Tideswell and he opened up a cycle repair business with his brother, (Markovitz Brothers). After several moves, to various premises around Tideswell, he purchased the site at the bottom of St. Johns Road in 1935 from the Tideswell and Millers Dale Coal and General Merchant Co., the business gradually developed into a Builders' Merchants. He never married and died in 1974 aged 86 years.

Joe Lomas Fletcher, the father of 17 children. He originated from Perry Foot, Peak Forest, in the early part of the century and lived on Wheston Bank. This picture was taken around 1920 displaying all his silverware won for his prize poultry.

Eric Simpson, born in Tideswell, was educated at Lady Manners School and later graduated in Architecture from Sheffield University.

After he did National Service in the R.A.F. he became an architect in Sheffield. He joined Chesterfield Borough Council, eventually becoming Borough Architect.

Eric will be remembered for his devotion to civic work and to Tideswell. He served on Tideswell Parish Council for 31 years and was Chairman for 19 years. He was the main instigator in the design and development of the Tideswell Sports Complex. He died, aged 62, in 1996.

Norman Gratton who was a very well respected member of the community during the twentieth century. He started work at Litton Mill when he was 13. He was a founder member of the Tideswell and District Co-operative Society, and was part time secretary, 1931-43. He instituted the purchase of the present Co-op building in 1920.

Further career details:

Justice of the Peace: 1939-1965.

Derbyshire County Council: 1938-1974. Alderman 1946; created Chairman in 1962-1965.

Labour Party Candidate for West Derbyshire 1950.

Peak Park Planning Board: 1952-1982; Chairman 1957-77.

C.B.E. for public service in Derbyshire: 1965. Degree of Master of Arts (Honorary) for Services to the Peak District National Park, (Sheffield University): 1977.

He died in 1982, aged 92 years.

And finally! Mrs. Lewis, Tideswell's Queen Mum, born November 5th 1900. This is her celebrating her 100th birthday. She first came to Tideswell in 1918, with her parents, when her father became Headmaster of the Council school in Parke Road.

Sheep and ox roasts seem to have been a popular form of entertainment in former years. This picture shows a sheep roast outside the Horse and Jockey Public House in the early part of the century.

Another view showing a sheep roast in Fountain Square.

The ox roast on the Queen's Coronation Day.

This is another scene of the ox roast on Coronation Day. The two girls are watching the ox being basted with great interest.

The loss of the Titanic evidently struck a chord across the whole community as the fund raising efforts of this unidentified group indicate.

St John's Girls Guild, New Year's Eve party – 1920s.

Thought to be a welcome home party for the survivors of the 1ˢᵗ World War in Tideswell C. of E. School. At the front is Mr Clarence Bramwell, who on demob from the Canadian Army, married and emigrated to Canada where he lived for over seventy years. He died in 1996 one week off his 100ᵗʰ Birthday.

Silver Jubilee celebrations outside the Ex Servicemen's Club, 1936.

Bonfire Night certainly involved many members of the community in the 1930s. This is the Town Head bonfire being built.

Members of Tideswell W.I. on an outing around 1960. Mr Brian Andrew, the coach driver, is on the top far left of the picture.

Mr Oliver Shimwell and helpers planting trees in the Fountain Garden to form the new setting for the welldressings in the early 1950s.

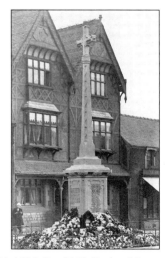

Above left: This was the dedication of the War Memorial on October 15th 1922. Dr. T. H. Parke, J.P. unveiled it. The Hunstone Brothers, monumental masons and woodcarvers of Tideswell, erected it.
Above right: A close-up photograph of the war Memorial.

Tideswell Cow Club Dinner at the Anchor Inn in the 1970s. **Back row:** Henry Radford; Peter Clayton; Dennis Tibbles; Don Gosney; Richard Furness; David Furness; Cecil Shirt. **Middle row:** Harry Making; Victor Gill; Harold Oven; Norman Gibbs; George Furness; Desmond Hall; George Needham. **Front row:** Wilfred Oven; Malcolm Robinson; Stanley Furness; George William Bull.

The Tideswell Cow Club have a tradition of planting a tree in memory of a recently deceased member. On this occasion they were planting the tree in memory of Mr Harry Making of Wheston.

We don't know what this occasion was, but the location is opposite Geil Torrs, and the workings were financed by Jim Brightmore (Patent Jim). After making some enquiries regarding the purpose of this project, we can only come up with some form of mineral extraction. The trench running up the hillside was for some kind of ventilation duct terminating in a chimney at the top.

King Hussein certainly created great interest when he arrived in his helicopter on the school playing field in 1995. Here he is surrounded by local people, who had come up to meet him. You might know Catherine Dalton would be there in the centre of the picture.

Left: H.R.H. Prince Philip, Duke of Edinburgh, on his visit to Tideswell on 29th May, 1984. He performed the official openings of the Industrial Estate on Whitecross Road (for the Development Commission), and the conversion into flats of the Old College in Market Square (for the Northern Counties Housing Association). It was a hot and sunny day and many fund raising events were held throughout the village.

Below: Prince Philip At the Old College conversion prior to unveiling the plaque.

This jolly group is located in Alley's Field in the 1950s. What, however, was the reason for the celebration, and who are the other people involved?

During the 20th century, Tideswell St. John's Ambulance Brigade always had a strong representation at most public events around the area. They disbanded during the 1990s.

Here they are standing to attention at an event at Staveley. From Left to right: Jim Morris; Harold Cartledge; Harold Grayson; Reg Flint; Wilf Oven; Jack Oliver; Reg Bingham.

Tideswell had a football team throughout the twentieth century, starting with the White Star Team.

They then had a team called The Red Star until the early 1920s. **Back row:** third from left is Mornington Cartledge, and on the right is Charlie Lowe. **Middle row:** on the right is Tommy Middleton. **Front row:** on the left is Walter Wood.

Then came the Blue Star which lasted until the late thirties. **Back row:** fourth from left is Bill Swindell. **Second row from front:** fourth from right is Tommy Middleton. **Front row:** second from left is Len Simpson.

Pictured are the 49rs football team who played in a charity football match against the 39rs in aid of the Tideswell Nursing Association. **Back Row:** Oswald How (quarryman); T.W. Handley (rate collector); Ivan Hill (insurance agent); Joe Dawson (overlooker at the weaving shed); Seth Harrison (wheelwright); Joe Brocklehurst (joiner & undertaker); Dr. Tom Parke(local G.P.); Mr. Broomhead (weaving shed worker). **Middle Row:** Tom Brocklehurst (painter); Dick Lomas (plasterer). **Front Row:** Capt. A.Brierley (bank manager); Hedley Bennet (railway signalman); Mr. Harrison (Litton Lane End Farm); Joe Dale (quarryman & Towncrier); Len Wagstaff (quarryman).

Tideswell Juniors around 1948. **Back Row:** Arnold Harrison; —; —; Derek Robinson; Rodney Rickets; Ronald Yates; John Hoare; Tant Sellars. **Middle Row:** Brian Hall; Derek Gibson; Alan Gratton. **Front Row:** Brian Andrew; Ken Flint; Ian Jones; Stan Gregory; Keith Repton.

The Derbyshire Medal Winning Team, 1949, photographed in front of The Derwent Arms, Bamford. **Back Row:** Stan Smith; Bill Riley; Fred Hambleton; Fred Dawson. **Next Row:** Peter Swarbrick; Joe Hambleton; Len Simpson; Bill Swindell; Tom Brocklehurst. **Next to front row:** Tommy Higginbottom; Walter Goucher; Alwyn Bradwell; Bateman Eyre; Jeff Naylor; Horace Tetsil. **Front Row:** Douglas Walton; Gordon Hallam; Harold Saunders; Gene Woodhouse; Hubert Walton.

Tideswell Football Team late 1940s. **Back Row:** Jeff Naylor; Harold Saunders; Fred Gilman; Bateman Eyre; Reg Paterson; Hubert Walton. **Front Row:** Gordon Hallam; Doug Walton; Horace Tetsil; Gene Woodhouse; Cliff Taylor.

Tideswell Football Team Early 1950s. **Back Row:** Bateman Eyre; Gordon Hallam; Jeff Naylor; Tommy Higginbottom; Harold Saunders; Peter Swarbrick; Bill Riley. **Front Row:** Horace Tetsil; Alwyn Bradwell; Walter Goucher; Gene Woodhouse; Cliff Taylor; Hubert Walton.

Tideswell Juniors Late 1950s. **Back Row:** Philip Motley; —; Ken Booth; John Ponsonby; Tony Robinson; Derry Gratton; Barry Case. **Front Row:** David Middleton; Lawrence Fletcher; —; Philip Spillane.

Tideswell Football Team around 1960. **Back Row:** Ken Booth; Horace Tetsil; Jeff Hambleton. **Middle Row:** John Lomas; Peter Drinkwater; Roy Middleton; John Turner; Peter Clayton; Peter Flint; David Booth; Lawrence Lomas. **Front Row:** David Flint; Colin Middleton; Terry Harrison; Colin Bowden; Nigel Bothamley.

Tideswell United around 1970. **Back row:** Frank Allan; Bill Swindell; Tony Middleton; Mick Hibbert; Julian Motley; Roy Ashton; Malcolm Bond; Andrew Hall; Derek Skidmore; Keith Furness; Warren Furness. **Front row:** Derek Parsons; Stephen Mellor; David Booth; Lol Middleton; John Middleton; Martin Butterworth.

Tideswell United 1st team. **Back row:** S. Hamilton; A. Bradbury; L. Harrison; L. Bradbury; T. Mitchell; S. Norris; M. Davies; S. Bingham; K. Furness. **Front row:** K. Yates; M. Bradbury; P. Jones; B. Hopkins; R. Lomas; M. Burke; S. Nash; J. White; D. Scott.

Tideswell United 2nd team. **Back row:** N. Willis; S. Beresford; L. Bennett; D. Hall; P. Jackson; D. Roberts; A. Greenan; D. Lockwood; I. Shirt. **Front row:** C. Killallea; A. Redfern; P. Andrew; B. Hopkins; R. Lomas; S. Amburey; P. Metcalf; R. Burton.

Tideswell had two bowling greens in the earlier part of the century, one behind the Belle Vue Public House, and another on Cliffe Lane. Here are two cup winning teams during the 1920s.

The opening ceremony of the Bowling Club at the new sports complex, 17th September, 1999.
Below right: The president of the club, Reg Bingham, bowling the first ball.

The cricket team during the 1950s. Third from the right on the back row is the Rev. Vere Ducker and on the front row, far left, is Mr. Turner the headmaster of Tideswell Pursglove School.

1960s cricket teams posing at the rear of Pursglove School.

The cricket team 2000 posing in front of the new pavilion.

Left: Another sport in which Tideswell excelled was bin-lid balancing. These are members of Tideswell Youth Club who beat Peak Dale Youth Club's record of twelve members standing on a dustbin lid. They managed to get fifteen of the members on the lid before the final collapse.

Chapter 6 – The Railway

Millers Dale Station had a very important part to play for the people of Tideswell and district until its closure in 1967. There was a regular station bus to pick up passengers for every train. This was formally owned and run by The George Hotel and then later by Bull's Coaches of Tideswell. Many local people used the train to travel to work in Buxton and at the time of its closure there were 19 journeys each way on weekdays.

With the enlargement of the station, to accommodate another two lines to make five platforms in all, a second viaduct was needed. Construction work was completed on 20th August 1905.

Passenger train and carriage at Miller's Dale.

General view of the Station with a goods train, south bound. The Station Master's house can just be seen above the steam of the engine. The Buxton train (push and pull) used platform five on the far left of the picture.

View of the station from the Buxton end, after it had closed, showing all five platforms.

Millers Dale Station signal box.

Above: The station in a state of dereliction, early 1970s.

Left: The two viaducts.

The station was the last one in England to have a post office on its platform. This is a copy of the postmark on the day of its closure, 4th March 1967.

The following photographs show a selection of local railway views. Monsal Viaduct became famous, nationally, after being pictured in Midland Railway publicity material.

The station at Bakewell would have been a familiar sight to Tideswell railway users.

The final images in this chapter show a section of line between Millers Dale and Buxton.

Steam trains on their way to Buxton through Ashwood Dale.

This is the Tideswell Male Voice Choir in full voice. Bob Armstrong; Dick Holmes, Harold Lewis, Roy Clay; Lionel Tanfield (on the piano); Lester Chapman; Raymond Hibbert and Ron Gaynor.

This is the Annual Baby Show, which usually took place in the Wesley Hall.

The annual Pantomime at the Congregational Chapel in the late 1940s. There were 47 people in the cast – not a bad turnout. How times have changed.

'Squirrel and his Nutters' were a group created for a bit of fun during the time that skiffle was at the height of its popularity in the late 50s. The leader was Cyril Warren. The Nutters consisted, mainly, of Congregational Chapel members. There weren't many musicians amongst them, but they certainly entertained and had fun.

'Squirrel and his Nutters' again.

Litton Minstrels.

Another view of Litton Minstrels.

These are the Congregational Church children practising for a singing event. Ken Thropp, at the back, is certainly giving everything he's got. Can you hear him?

The Wesleyan Chapel also gave some good shows and pantomimes.
This is one of them around 1947.

Tideswell used to have The Maureen Cardno School of Dancing from the late 1940s to the mid
1950s. It was very well attended and they put on many shows and exhibitions. They trained and
practised in the Belle Vue clubroom. The dancers, here, are in the Market Square on Carnival
Day about 1950.

The Maureen Cardno Dancers shown during Wakes Festivities.

British Legion party 1957, the guests on the nearest table from left to right are: Jane Kenworthy; Nellie Willis; Mr. And Mrs. Bernard Brocklehurst; Mr. and Mrs. Frank Watkins.

The Over Sixties Choir dating from around 1965. What a smart group!

Church Walk hymn singing outside the Belle Vue.

An early photograph showing a Coronation Day street party.

A Jubilee bonfire party on Wheston Bank.

A guising group from the late 1920s.

Chapter 8 – Floods and Snow

Being one thousand feet above sea level, Tideswell has had its fair share of extreme weather conditions. Over the last century we have photographic evidence of various floods and snow scenes.

These are scenes from August 1912 outside The Bull's Head looking up Commercial Road.

This scene, of the fireman and the child onlookers, shows the three storey building adjoining the Co-op which was demolished in the 1950s for the road widening scheme around the Bank Corner.

Franco Abreu, Judith Mount and Allison Bell surveying the scene outside the Madeira House Restaurant and Tideswell Stores.

Jim Hadfield, doing a good job of work, helping the floodwater on its way outside the church.

The floodwater making its way down Manchester Road from Brook Bottom.

Mr Douglas Chapman opening the church gates to let the water out of the churchyard.

Paul Mount having fun delivering milk outside The Old College.

Above: Looking up the village from the bus shelter on Buxton Road.
Right: This is a scene on the Water Cum Jolly road between Litton Mill and Cressbrook Mill.
Below: Two motor vehicles passing near to the Picnic Area.

Tideswell Moor February 14th, 1947.

A scene on the main road looking towards the Anchor Inn on 14th January, 1987.

Terrace Road 1991. Yes! there are motor vehicles under the snow on the right of the picture.

The same place, but looking in the opposite direction on Terrace Road.

Looking down towards Tideswell from Wheston Bank in 1991.

A winter scene showing the George Hotel and the church in January 1987.

A winter scene of the Church taken from Cliffe Lane, year unknown.

Snow scene at Wardlow.

Group of local people walking up the main road in Wardlow in 1947. From left to right are: Doris Turner; Christine Jackson; Norah Jackson; George Jackson; June Turner; Ellen Haslam; Pheobe Armitt; Brian Armitt; the man leading the horse is George Haslam.

Charlie Armes on Alma Road

The old Guildhall had reached a rather dilapidated state structurally. It was replaced by the present building on the same site. This photograph dating from 1905, shows the partly constructed building. The main contractor for this undertaking was Roland Hill pictured (with white beard) in the right centre background.

Jabez Slack and his workmen posing in front of their premises, Lawson Cottage, in the early part of the 20th century. They used to sell building materials, and had facilities at their premises for turning lumplime (which was obtainable from local limekilns) into putty lime. This was used for building and plastering and also for whitewashing walls and ceilings which would be the equivalent of our emulsion paint of today. The lime was sold at tuppence for a bucket full.

Construction work on the new Pursglove School in 1937. **Back Row:** Arnold Marshal; Bill Evans; Walter Moor; Frank Hill; **Front Row:** Cameron Hill; Bill Shenton; Bob Bartlet; Tommy Jones.

Builders Cameron, Archie and Frank Hill in 1937, commencing the groundwork of the pair of houses opposite Darkbrook Pianos' showroom and workshop.

Of course Tideswell had its own share of defending to do during the 1939-45 war. This picture shows the construction of the Home Guard Post at the top of Summer Cross. Dr. Brookes can be seen supervising through the window.

During our investigations a number of group photographs of workers have come to light. The photograph above shows staff, managers and shareholders of the Co-op, taken in the late 1920s.

Above: This is the combined workforce of the Velvet Mill posing on Manchester Road, outside the mill, in the early part of the century. This, in due course, became Swift Levick's and currently Holdsworth's.

Left: Inside the Weaving Shed celebrating the Coronation of George VI. Here are some of the workers we can identify.
Back row: Nellie Firth (Walker); Marion Robinson; Edith Cartledge; Connie Brown (Duncan); Barbara Skidmore.
Front Row: Connie Mullins; Renie Brassington.

Swift Levick's workforce just before the factory closed down in 1970s. The photograph was taken by Harry Ball using the time exposure technique. He is seen posing extreme front right of the group.

The Parish Council dating from the early 1960s. The personnel include Dr Culshaw, Elsie Frost; Ken Gibson; Eva Brightmore; Bill Swindell; Fred Slack; John Lythgoe; Geoff Naylor; Bill Laurence.

Two views showing council workers laying kerbs at the Anchor Crossroads in 1950. This was part of the road kerbing scheme from Stoney Middleton Dale to Peak Forest from the late 1940s to the early 1950s. The junction was staggered in the early 1960s after a series of motor accidents, some fatal.

County Council workers and other notables involved in the road widening of Commercial Road in 1958. Many graves had to be dug up and the bones removed and placed in separate timber caskets for reburial in the churchyard. The graveyard was screened with canvas for privacy. The workers received an extra sixpence an hour for the privilege. The King's Head was also demolished in the same scheme. **Back Row:** Brian Purser; Harry Bingham; Rudi ?; Bill Bagguley; Len Turner; Oliver Shimwell (Headmaster of Cof E School); Douglas Chapman; Frank Riley; John Naylor; William Hunstone; Graham Hollinsworth. **Front Row:** Graham Haslam; –; Frank Akers (D.C.C. District Building Surveyor); Rev. Vere Ducker; Norman Gratton; Robert Blunt (surveyor); –.

Theophilus Mycock with the horse and cart belonging to Thomas Dakin of Millers Dale. Dakin's later owned a steam lorry for transport duties.

These two pictures show Frank Frost the handyman/gardener for Dr Parke and, later, Dr Brookes (who lived at Foxlow House). The photographs show his transition from horse to internal combustion power. The motor car is reputed to be the first one in Tideswell.

A railway gang working on the Millers Dale line.

Harold Walker with show horse, Cwyfan. A lasting memorial to this animal is provided by naming his house in Cherry Tree Square after it. The house is now occupied by Harold's daughter and family.

Above: Palfreyman's, was situated opposite the church. It was obviously a very busy shop judging by the range of wares it carried.

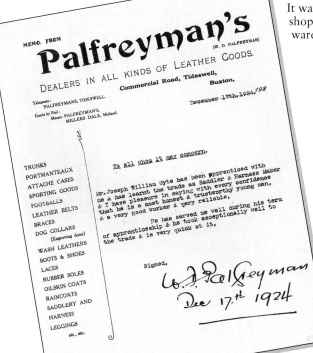

Left: The related document refers to the completion of the apprenticeship of Mr Joseph Gyte at Palfreyman's in the trade of Saddler and Harness Maker.

Left: Frank Chapman whose workshop was housed in the premises currently occupied by the Hills'n'Dales Tea Room. Chapman's occupied the premises from the early 1920s having taken over the use of the building from the Lomas family who were builders and joiners in the late 19th and early 20th century.

Frank Chapman and his sons, Esplin, Jim, Frank and Joe were joiners and undertakers. Frank worked until well into his 80s specialising in oak furniture in his latter years.

Below: Joe, his son, pictured below, was the last of the Chapman brothers to work in the shop. He continued until the late 1980s, when he retired.

Another well known village craftsman was Bill Hunstone, the third generation and the last professional woodcarver of the famous family in Tideswell. The family was originally in building and stonemasonry, but Advent Hunstone, in the latter part of the 19th century, found he had a gift for woodcarving and ecclesiastical design and broke away from the family trade. Their work can be found all round the locality. Bill was a very well respected member of the community; it's a shame that the changing times and priorities of the community restrict the demand for the Hunstone's type of work.

Bill Hunstone's father William Hunstone. He was the son of Advent Hunstone.

Right: Norman Gibbs who is the owner of the last butcher's shop in Tideswell. Here he is carving the round of beef for the Cow Club Supper at the George Hotel in 1975.

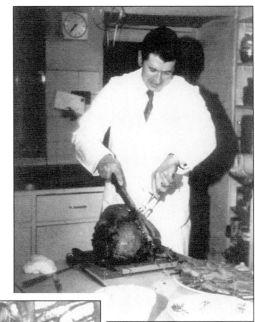

Left: Another familiar scene in Tideswell. A travelling knife and scissor grinder at work on Lower Terrace Road in the 1970s.

Bill Bagshaw, on his Ferguson T20 tractor in winter, during the late 1950s.

Eddie Kenworthy standing outside his workshop, which was situated adjacent to The First Drop Inn, now Rockingham Lodge, in Market Square. He served his apprenticeship with his Uncle, Bernard Brocklehurst of Tideswell. He retired in January 1998, and was Tideswell's last undertaker.

Left: Two unidentified workers at Millers Dale Quarry.

Below: A photograph of Arnold Walker, farmer.

Mrs Miriam Chapman, watched by her colleagues from Tideswell Post Office, as she sets off on her last round, after 23 years of service.

Tideswell, in common with most English villages, was able, at one time, to provide a much greater selection of hostelries than at present. The first selection of photographs show some of the pubs which have now disappeared or have undergone a change of use.

Above: The Cross Daggers Inn stood where the current Ex Servicemen's Club now stands. The building, pictured, burned down in 1937.

Left: The King's Head (demolished 1958) stood to the right, as one exited the main gates of the church yard.

Opposite The King's Head and adjacent to Tideswell Stores was The Bull's Head, now a private dwelling.

The Three Tuns Inn, in the background of the picture, was in the Market Square. It is now a private dwelling. The front façade has changed little since the photograph was taken.

Similarly, the building that was formally The Miner's Arms in Church Street seems little altered from that shown in the photograph. William Yates the landlord is standing at the door.

The George Hotel during the infamous 1947 snow.

These two pictures, showing charabanc excursions, provide excellent views of The George and The Horse and Jockey public houses. Presumably the character, on the right of the photograph of The George, was there to provide some form of travelling entertainment.

The Anchor Inn has not dramatically changed since these photographs were taken.

The Belle Vue Hotel stood in the Market Square in Tideswell. It was subsequently renamed The First Drop Inn which many will remember providing lively Thursday evening entertainment for the residents who lived in the Market Square.

The Railway Hotel, Millers Dale, was rather a grand establishment earlier this century when the railways were in their heyday. It was subsequently renamed the Dale Hotel after the closing of the station in 1967. It has now been converted into two private dwellings.

This was The Bull's Head at Monsal Head, situated on the same site as the Monsal Head Hotel is today.

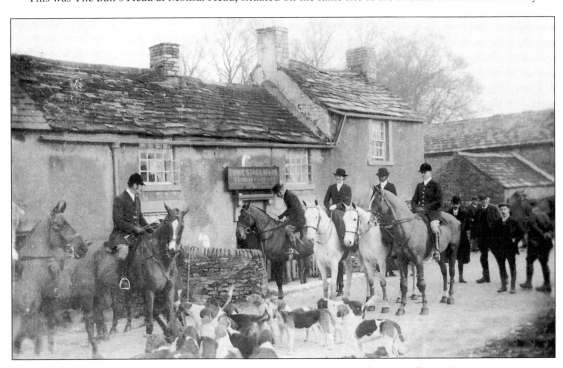

The High Peak Harriers outside The Three Stags Heads at Wardlow Mires.

Above: The Ball Inn (now demolished), Stoney Middleton Dale, situated at the junction of Eyam Dale and Middleton Dale. The site is now used as a car park for the quarry opposite.

Left: We could not locate a picture of the Peacock Hotel in Tideswell. This picture is of the last tenants, Freddie and Connie Lomas Fletcher, standing behind their bar. They also bred and raced greyhounds and raised beagles for the hunt. The picture was taken on the day they retired, in 1973, having being tenants for 36 years.

The property was later sold and converted to a private residence.

Above: Tideswell May Queen 1908-09, Nellie Walton (Mrs Graham Gilbert), outside Foxlow House, Sherwood Road.

Left: Another early carnival picture shows what looks like a Welsh tea party scene on a dressed up hay cart at the end of Sherwood Road. The gentleman attending the horse seems to be taking it all very seriously.

Tideswell's first welldressing, 1946. On the far right is Oliver Shimwell, the leading light of the group. He originated from Youlgreave. His family were well established in welldressing before the war and, thankfully, he brought the tradition and the know how with him when he became Headmaster of Tideswell Church of England Primary School. **From left to right:** Reg Bingham; Esplin Chapman; Syd Goodwin; Ernest Warren; Arthur Gratton; Joe Watson; Sam Flint; Oliver Shimwell.

The ladies of the first Wakes Committee, posing around the first welldressing. **Left to right:** Dora Hill; Ivy Bingham; Rene Locke; Mary Simpson; Betty Chapman; Ruth Robinson; Maggie Walton; Sarah Chapman; Edna Wood; Eva Fletcher.

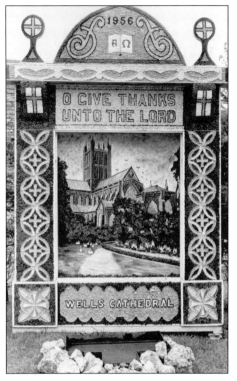

Above left and right: A selection of welldressings from the late 1950s
Below: The welldressing service in 1950.
Opposite page: The welldressing of Tideswell Church in 1950.

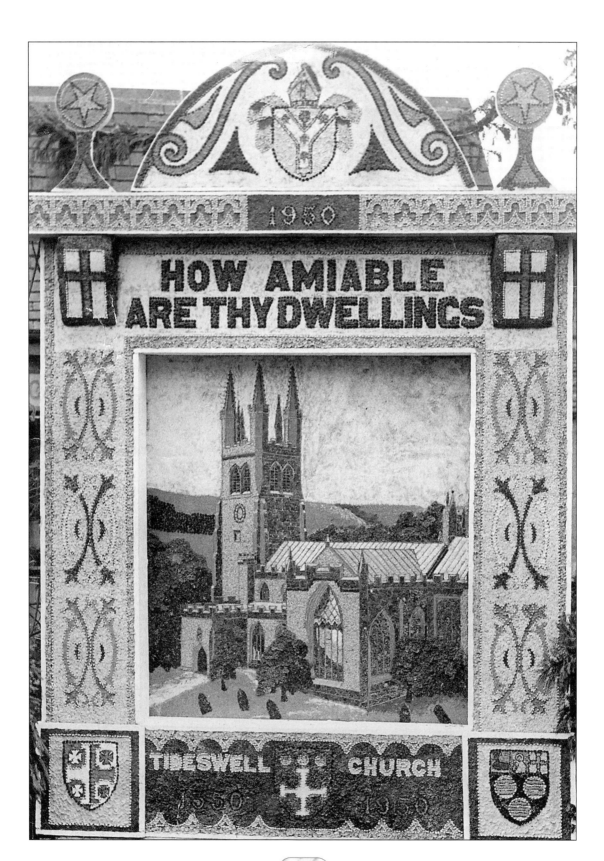

The following photographs represent a selection of the welldressings in the 1960s.

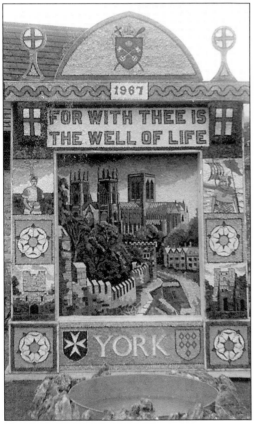

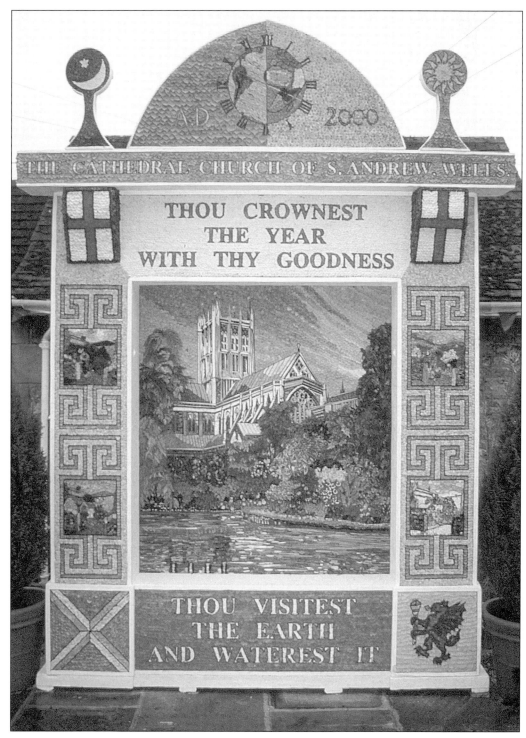

Tideswell welldressing for the millennium. The colours were really stunning.

Tideswell Majorettes in the early 1950s.

Tideswell Majorettes from the 1960s.

Tideswell Majorettes, 1959. A fine array of Tidza talent. Note the cut off, painted wellingtons they are wearing. **Back row:** Valerie Beard; Dorothy Robinson; Susan Newbound; Diane Lomas; Olive Shaw; Yvonne Slack; June Duncan; Joan Oven; Gloria Marshall. **Front row:** Dianne Flint; Judith Garner; Anita Godden; Margaret Swindell; Gwen Hattersley; Margaret Crookes.

Tideswell Wakes Dancers in action, around 1990. The three happy girls featured are: Kathy Whitehouse; Becky Holland and Faye Mellor.

Tidza Saw-Yeds in the early 1950s. **Left to right:** Terry Yates; Dennis Dawes; Clive Marsden; Harry Shirt; Archie Hill. Joe Chapman wrote his Tidza-Saw-Yeds rhyme for this event. It was placed in the windows of the Ford V 8 shooting-brake.

The float of the members of the Congregational Youth Organization (C.Y.O.) from about 1950.
Back left: Joyce Robinson; Marian Swindell; Joyce Middleton; Jean Moseley; Mildred Walton.
Front left: Rene Heath; Margaret Gilbert; Marian Swarbrick.

Johnnie Allsop's pickup coming up Church Street in the 1940s. The carnival was the highlight of the year for many people in those days, as can be seen from this picture (on a wet day).

Margaret Watson (Hall) posing in the Old Grammar School yard in the late 1940s. Just marvel at the number of attendants in her retinue.

Barbara Leach, the 1953 carnival queen, with her retinue at the crowning ceremony.

Barbara and her retinue on the float on Sherwood Road.

Armand and Michaela Dennis made a brief appearance at a 1960s wakes procession.

This is an early 1950s children's group posing in the Market Square. Note the sign over the shop window: 'For Your Throats Sake Smoke Craven A.'

Tideswell's Comic Band, late 1950s. They were usually represented in the 1950s and 1960s carnival processions.

Glamorous Grandmother competitions used to be very popular. Here is Mrs Edith Leach, the Glamorous Grandmother of 1961.

A picture of the Litton maypole dancers around 1960. **Back row:** Lynne Beresford; Wanda Louzskin; Carol Armstrong; Anne Gratton; Marilyn Slack; Christina Oldfield; Merlyn Saunders; Sonia Bates; Kathryne Campbell. **Front row:** Susan Campbell; Anna Louzskin; Anne Hall; Beryl Saunders; Helen Campbell; Margaret Saunders.

Tideswell Maypole Dancers in the 1950s. Jessie Oldfield and Florence Walker the trainers. **Back row:** Audrey Harrison; Denise Brightmore; Maurine Boam; —; Marjory Clayton. **Middle Row:** Peggy Pennock; —; Judith Scard; Sheila Robinson; —; **Front row:** Dianne Gibson; Silvia Hambleton; Anne Watkins; Brenda Bowyer.

This wonderful photograph shows Canon Fletcher and others posed on the steps of the Vicarage. Circa 1900.

These children were the Tideswell C. of E. choirs competing in the Buxton Music Festival of 1925.

The charabanc photograph depicts members of the church choir trip to Blackpool in August 1925.
They arrived back in Tideswell at 3.00a.m on Sunday.

Tideswell Parish Churchworkers Gathering. Tideswell Church could certainly obtain the services of a great many parishioners in the early part of the century. There are well above a hundred people posing in front of Tideswell Church of England School.

Oct 4th 1953. Dedication of the new Coronation Gates, Tideswell Church. **Left to right:** Mr Derbyshire of Baslow, who made the gates and post; Mr Advent Hunstone, of Tideswell who designed the gates; Frank Lomas, from Baltimore, U.S.A. who originated from Tideswell, assisted; Rev. Vere Townsend Ducker, who dedicated the gates; and Mr Benjiman Lomas Fletcher, Chairman of Tideswell Parish Council, who declared them open.

Tideswell Congregational Church Choir, 1910.

This is the Tideswell Congregational Sunday School Walk in the Market Square. The Churches of Tideswell always had a Sunday School Walk during the Wakes Week. The church walked on one day and the chapels combined on their walk. Both walks had Tideswell Band in attendance.

Here we have the Sunday School Procession in Queen Street in 1907.

Almost the same view. However a different section of the Procession is shown.

The Sunday School Procession in Fountain Square having stopped at one of many places for the hymn singing. Note the organ being played on the back of the cart.

Tideswell Congregational Church New Sunday School opened 29th April, 1939, by Mr Henry B. Saint, of Newcastle. This replaced the old Council School building, which was of a similar size in plan, but a two storey building. Mr Baker was last Headmaster of the school when it closed around 1936.

These panoramic views taken in front of the George Hotel, in the 1930s, show the Chapel Walk. The group have stopped for hymn singing. It is interesting to note that these images were unable to be joined to make one photograph due to the exposures being taken several minutes apart. See the band member in the background who has turned around to his left.

Chapter 13 – School

In the first part of the 20th century, Tideswell was well served with educational establishments. It had the Grammar School, which had been in existence since 1560 and was closed in 1932. It had the Council School, which was situated in the United Reform School Room at the top of Parke Road, (this closed in 1936). It also had the Church of England School, which has recently been converted into dwellings. Tideswell Pursglove was opened as a Secondary Modern School in 1936. It continued until 1974 when it became the Bishop Pursglove Primary School. The secondary children were transferred to Lady Manners School, Bakewell.

Tideswell Grammar School (1908), taken in front of Blake House. The headmaster in those days was Dr. W.G.Boule. He was assistant master from 1887 to 1894, then became Headmaster until 1917.

A Council School group, in the early 1900s (mainly non-conformists). Mr Hadfield is the Headmaster. He retired in 1918 when Mr. Baker took over.

Above left: Shrove Tuesday, Church of England School, Barring Out. This was an ancient custom. Children who were generally late for school were carried shoulder high on a pole by their school mates crying out, "We dar-ner bar im art", to the tune of "For he's a jolly good fellow". In the background is the Ex Servicemen's Club formerly the Cross Daggers Inn. **Above right:** Mr W.H.Baker the Headmaster of the Council School from 1919 to 1936 (when the school closed down). He was nick-named 'Banty' Baker because of his great interest in these birds.

Council School pupils 1920s. **Back row left to right:** Muriel Turner; Ethel Hill; Eric Gratton; Brenda Cross; Victor Hall; Lily Mosely; Tom Turner; Dora Gratton; Alison Redfern. **2nd row:** Bessie Heath; Edna Jackson; Bill Gratton; Jean Pritchard; Delilah Jackson; Thelma Owen; Nellie Furness; Muriel Walton; Beatrice Walker. **Front Row:** Jim Slack; Ken Quigley; Clifford Smith; Harold Mycock; Douglas Walton.

Church of England School, 1948, 5 and 6 year olds. **Left to right back row:** Jeffrey Mabbot; Tony Hill; Judith Gratton; Elizabeth Black; Hazel Barber; Maureen Marshall; Glenys Beard; Marjory Clayton; Dorothy Robinson; Barry Lomas; Michael Hattersley; Keith Shaw. **Middle Row:** Bill Duncan; Jackie Williams; Anne Hattersley; Sheila Robinson; Christine Davies; —; Pamela Hambleton; Carol McGuinness; Audrey Harrison; Erica Throppe; Jeff Hadfield. **Front Row:** Harold Oven; Barry Taylor; George Smith; Ron Cartledge; Richard Gregory; Peter Chappell; Arnold Crookes; David Thorpe; Malcolm Burns; Trevor Walker.

A Bishop Pursglove class photograph from around 1974. **Back row:** Paul Gosling; Shaun Stoddart; Andrew Fletcher; Peter Ashton; Julie Middleton; Clare Brocklehurst; David Hopkins. **Next row:** Melody Hadjipetrou; Robert Hill; Michael Bond; Christopher Pearson; —; Robinson; —; Jeanette Buckley **Next row:** —; Clare Bates; Sara & Louise Roberts; Mathew Warburton; Devina Sellars; Mark Robson; Mark Allen **Front row:** Chris Flint; Sally Anne Andrew; Neil Harding; David Shimwell; Susan Wilson.

This photograph shows Mrs Kathryn Black's class at Pursglove School in the 1980s.
Back row: Carl Mellon; Marie Hallows; Matthew Lythgoe; Tania Lomas Fletcher; Jane Hadfield; James Shirt; Lee Bothamley. **Middle row:** —; Caroline Croll; Rachael Saxby; Louise Ponsonby; Tracy Flint; Antonia Hunstone; Ivan Jensen. **Front row:** Joanne Green; Sharon Newton; Julian Hallam; Joanne Bothamley; John Wright; Mark Howard; Michael Bower.

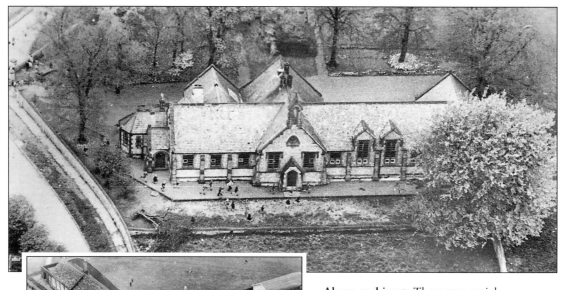

Above and inset: These two aerial photographs show the primary and secondary schools in Tideswell prior to the transfer of primary pupils to Pursglove School and the transfer of secondary pupils to Lady Manners School, Bakewell.

Above and inset: Two views of the same entrance drive to Bishop Pursglove School showing progressive development in this area.

No social history of Tideswell would be complete without reference to the amateur dramatics group associated with the village. T.C.P. productions have been a regular feature of village life for many years.

Mrs Annie Scholefield founded the players in 1930, with the assistance of many like-minded friends. In 1931, under her auspices, it became the Community Players as part of Derbyshire Rural Community Council's efforts to broaden the interests and enhance the lives of rural communities, who had little access to live theatre.

During the World War II the Players raised funds for numerous charities. Mrs Scholefield corresponded with many funding agencies, benefactors, and some playwrights. Several plays had their first public performances by the Players in Tideswell. Those who had the privilege of working with her appreciated her thoroughness in rehearsals, her knowledge of stage craft and her absolute dedication as director to THE PLAY.

Cock a Doodle Doo was a 1967 production featuring: Edith Southwell; Jane Bennett; Ron Burton; Colin Moseley; Mary Ayers; Marion Mellor and Dennis Southwell.

Look Out for the Catch dates from 1968. It featured: Edgar Shaw, Ken Gilbert; Don Ayers; Dorothy Furness; John Hallows; Helen Flint; Jennifer Tricklebank; Barbara Holdsworth and Ron Daybell.

The following is a fairly comprehensive list of the productions by T.C.P. over the years. The Players continue to enjoy considerable success and support. They played to full houses during the recent production of *When we are Married*. The following pages show a selection of photographs of productions and casts.

193?	The Barton Mystery		1955	Letter from the General
1931	Silas Marner			Down to Brass Tacks
1932	Chesterfield–One Act Festival–It is			Two One Act Plays
	Written		1956	Cock-a-Doodle-Doo
1933	The Bells–One Act–Sad About Europe			Ten Little ——
1934	Britannia of Billingsgate			Three One Acts
1935	Outward Bound		1957	House on the Cliff
1936	????			Look Out for the Catch
1937	The Ghost Train			Pantomime–Jack and the Beanstalk
1938	Third Time Lucky–Four On Acts		1958	The Sound of murder
1939	The Wreckers			My Three Angels
1940	Billeted			Three One Acts
1942	Laburnum Grove		1959	Shock Tactics
1943	Once Bitten Twice Shy			Search By Night
	Doctor, There's a Danger		1960	Busy Body
1944	The Man Who Changed His Name			Post Horn Gallup
	The Brass Door Knob		1961	Arsenic & Old Lace
1945	Ladies in Waiting–Two One Acts		1962	The Mystery of the Marie Celleste
1946	The Blue Goose			Pantomime–Robinson Crusoe
1949	Money		1963	Caesar's Friend
	The Hasty Heart		1977	But Once a Year
	Black Limelight		1978	Pantomime–Ali Bab
1950	Way of the Cross		1980	Wait Until Dark
	Miss Mabel		198?	The Thwarting of Barry Bolingrew
	Quiet Weekend		1981	She's Done it Again
	One Act–Copper Kettle		1983	See How They Run
1951	Ghost Train		1984	Death Trap
	Ten Little ——		1985	Cat On the fiddle
1952	Bonaventure		1986	Sailor Beware
	Happiest Days of our Lives			My Giddy Aunt
1953	Square Pegs		1987	Pantomime–Tidzarella
1955	Chinese Bungalow		1988	Panic Stations
	Job for the Boys			Gaslight
	Shrove Tuesday Concert		1989	Running Riot
	One Acts–Great Hucklow			The Murder room
	Wakes Concert		1990	An Inspector calls
	Wormhill		1991	Table Manners
	Wardlow			Pot Pourri Two Ona Acts
	Litton			A Tomb With a View
1956	Off the Deep End		1992	Night Must Fall
1957	The Offending Hand			Relatively Speaking
1958	The Peaceful Inn		1993	Play On
	Queen Elizabeth Slept Here			One Acts
	Parish Church–Play In Verse Good Friday			Pantomime–Ali Baba
1959	Dr. Morrelle		1994	House Guests
	Dry Rot			The Happiest days of your Life
1960	The Cat and the Canary		1995	Joking Apart
	Man for the Job			Pantomime–Snow White
1961	Treasure on Pelican			Sadata–One Acts
	Breath of Spring			One Acts
	Two One Acts		1996	Look Who's Talking
1962	The Whole Truth			Habeas Corpus
	Haul for the Shore		1997	Outside Edge
	Two One Acts		1998	Suddenly at Home
1963	The Vigil			Educating Rita
	Wanted One Body			Pantomime–Miss Muffet
	Pot-Pourri–One Acts		1999	Pantomime–Aladdin
1964	The Unexpected Guest			Three One Acts
	Strike Happy			Sadata–OneAct
	Two One Acts			Murdered to Death
1965	So Many Children		2000	Up and Under
	Too Soon for Daisies			
	Pantomime–Aladdin			Proposed next play: When We are Married

Above: *Letter from the General* dates from 1966, featuring from left to right; Barbara ?; Eric Simpson; Edith Southwell; Renee Thropp; John Mount; Dorothy Furness; Mary Ayers; Carol Knott; Dennis Southwell.

Left: This photograph features Norman Gregory; Ron Cartledge; Brenda Ponsonby; Eileen Gilbert; Dorothy Furness; Edgar Shaw.

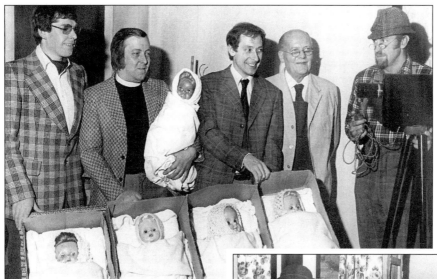

Above: This photograph features: Keith Furness; Mark Lythgoe; Paul Fletcher and Adrian Dawson.

Right: *She's Done it Again* dating from 1981, featured: Ted Shimwell; Miriam Sellars; Debbie Shaw; Kathryn Black; and Charles Houlton.

Below: The photograph of the cast of *Tidzarella* shows: Clive Fell; John Worwood; John Marriott; Lindsey Bond; —; Rebeccah Jackson; Polly Jensen; Iain Burnett; Jannine Croll; —; —; Helena Howell; —; —; and Paul Black.

Tideswell Band is one of the great 'institutions' of the village. There can be few really significant community events which have not involved the band in some way. The earliest image of Tideswell Band dates from 1909. We cannot identify the bandsmen from this date, but we note the quality of the uniform and the looks of pride on many of the faces of those photographed.

This photograph dates from approximately 1945. The personnel include: Mornington Cartledge; Tom Skidmore; Bernard Broklehurst; Cecil Lawrence; Bill Lawrence; Frank Frost; Frank Bagshaw; Bill Skidmore; Frank Bradbury; Lawrence Swift; Roy Gibson.

This photograph, like the one which follows, dates from the 1950s. It includes: Bob Banks; Doug Andrews; Lionel Bagshaw; Vernon Watson; Eddie Kenworthy; Lawrence Swift; Bernard Brocklehurst; Tom Skidmore; Richard Tibbles; Derek Shaw; Roy Gibson; Ted Brocklehurst; Frank Bagshaw; Jack Bradbury; John Lomas Fletcher and, on the drum, Colin Moseley.

The final band photograph shows some of the same personnel as the previous picture. However, we have been able to identify a few other bandsmen in this group including Jack Hambleton, Derek Skidmore and Peter Furness.

Chapter 16 – Surrounding Villages

The following photographs derive from local villages surrounding Tideswell.

Cressbrook

Above: The school photograph of 1938 shows pupils from the former Cressbrook Primary School. The teacher is Verna Brett (Goodwin). Verna taught there from 1938 to 1945. During the war years there were many evacuees from Manchester who were housed with families in Cressbrook and, at times, the school had up to 40 pupils.

Right: This photograph of Cressbrook Church shows this building before a dwelling was constructed to the left.

This dark scene has changed little since the picture was taken; it is of course Ravensdale Cottages, often rather quaintly referred to as 'Bury-me-Wick'.

This is a finely posed image of Post Office Row at Cressbrook.

Above: This view, although hazy, shows the buildings clustered behind the mill. The mill is now being redeveloped, and many changes are now taking place.

Above and inset: The Upper and Lower Lodges at Cressbrook Hall.

The shop at Cressbrook, dated 1919. It later became part of the Tideswell and District Co-op and closed some time in the 1970s and is now a private residence.

This is a group photograph of the staff of The Columbia Picture Corporation celebrating their ninth anniversary. They were transferred to Cressbrook Hall during the war years from 1940 to 1946. Whilst they were here they employed a number of local people. Those we have identified are: Patsy Pitt; Eva Shaw (Fletcher); Lillian Harrison; Joyce Lomas (Baker); Joyce Allen; Syd Baker; Marian Bennett.

This photograph dates from around 1920 and shows pupils from Great Hucklow School.

The cyclist and friend are standing on the road from Great Hucklow to Windmill.

Above: This view shows the lane leading to Great Hucklow School. This lane formed part of the Sheffield to Buxton turnpike road. **Inset:** Eva and Mary Maltby posing in the school playground. Eva married Vernon Brightmore of Tideswell. **Below:** Great Hucklow Oddfellows posed for this picture outside the Queen Ann on their annual parade day.

This is a fine view of Litton Mill showing the rear of Curzon Terrace. The water from the River Wye is dammed up to form the lake to provide power for the water wheel to run the mill.

The mill lake and footbridge at Litton Mill.

This scene, at Litton, shows a much less wooded view down the main street than the present one.

Litton people certainly went to town when they constructed this highly decorative archway to the newly opened Working Men's Club.

This photograph shows the former mill, in Millers Dale, in the foreground. This was called Tideswell Mill because it was in the Tideswell Parish; it closed in the 1920s. The mill was known as the Meal Mill and it ground oats. The old tearoom, which closed in the 1960s, is on the opposite side of the main road.

This view of Tideswell Mill gives a good idea of the size and location of the millpond.

This later photograph of Millers Dale shows the Tea Room and the gable end of Tideswell Mill.

Millers Dale village.

Above left and right: These two pictures are a later view of Tideswell Mill. It was demolished in the 1970s to make a site for a water pumping station for the North Derbyshire Water Board.

An idyllic photograph dated 1908. The old gentleman with his horse and cart must have been a familiar site to the many Tideswell travellers making their way to the station in those far off days. Take note of the mill in the background. This was the other mill in Millers Dale. It was known as the Wormhill Mill being situated in that parish. Both mills were owned by the same family, the Dakins. The mills were sold to Staffordshire Farmers in 1949. This mill was still water driven until the mid 1950s.

Left and below:
Staffordshire Farmers' workmen in the 1950s. The work men in the lower photograph are, left to right: George Mycock and Ernest Hollingdrake (mill workers); Cliff Hancock (traveller); Peter Cartledge (worked in the office); Dennis Pedley (lorry driver).

An unusual aerial photograph of Millers Dale.

This scene would have been familiar to generations of Tideswell travellers as they made their way to Millers Dale to catch trains to and from the famous station.

These two general views show part of the station and the quarry on the hillside.

This is an unusual view of Millers Dale showing the station at the top right of the picture, and the road leading to Buxton.

A 1930s view showing the Old Road to Tideswell and the Tearoom on the left.

Above: A mother and child posing on the road in Millers Dale, with the mill and a dramatic sky in the background. Note the road, prior to tarmac, with the pile of stone chippings for mending the potholes.

Inset: This photograph shows a view along the road from Millers Dale to Litton Mill. The pose appears a little 'stiff'.

below: A much more artistic view of the same area.

This delightfully posed photograph shows the bridge and church in Millers Dale.

This must have been a familiar scene around the turn of the century. Mother and children taking a stroll along the road.

This photograph shows the pedestrian route to Monsal Dale Station.

An interesting illustration with a rather out of scale passenger train superimposed on the
Monsal Dale viaduct.

Even in earlier days Monsal Head was a favourite viewpoint for the valley below.

Ravenstor Youth Hostel was built as a private residence for Mr Peter Dickie, the part owner of both Litton and Cressbrook Mills.

The Ball Inn at the junction of Eyam Dale and Stoney Middleton Dale. There is also a good view of Stoney Middleton Dale where you can clearly see the spoil heaps left over from the lime kilns and the lead smelting mills that were part of the scenery of the nineteenth century.

You certainly could not stop to have your photograph taken, on what is now the busy main street of Stoney Middleton.

Above: Wardlow welldressing, 1972. In commemoration of the church's centenary year. Left to right: Joan Richardson; Barbara and Michael Robinson; Bertha Furness; Nora Jackson; Joe Bagshaw and Tom Bandy.

Above left: George Edward Haslam with his catch for the morning. He used to work for the Bridges and Highways Department of the County Council, but, in his spare time, he was the man the farmers informed of any foxes seen in the area of Wardlow. Out just before daybreak to wait for the fox to come out of its lair, his favourite haunt was Ravensdale Wood where many of the foxes were shot. He also caught moles and used to sell the dried skins. **Above right:** Joseph and Margaret Simpson at Hall Farm.

This is a view at the rear of Grange Farm, Wheston.

Stewart Making and Bill Duncan on an Allis Chalmers tractor in the late 1950s.

A street scene at Wormhill looking up the village towards the school.

A view of the Bagshaw Arms in Wormhill, taken from Glebe Farm.

This photograph is a real period piece showing the Wormhill Home Guard 1942-43, Personnel include: Joe Mellor; ? Thompson; Bill Skidmore; Henry Mellor; Frank Beresford; Stan Teeboon; Sonny Bowler; Jack Lambert; Tommy Teeboon Snr; —; Tommy Teeboon; Les Wilshaw; Ted Simpson. Not a bad turnout for a small village.

The Brindley Fountain and Post Office in the early 1900s.

Above left and right: Two views showing the new Sports Complex during development.

The family and friends of Abigail Marcus at the opening of the children's playground. This development is dedicated to the memory of Abigail Marcus, a valued and popular child of our community. The fundraising, design and construction of this playground was organised by the family and friends of Abigail. It has proved a popular attraction!

Tale of "Tidza"

Now we know that we are called 'Saw-Yeds' by residents of the surrounding villages, we thought we'd end the book with our very own legend in rhyme.

A TALE OF "TIDZA"

One day near June the twenty-fourth, four Tidza farmers sallied forth,
To free a cow that cruel fate, had fastened in a five-barred gate.
With ropes and axes, picks and saws, they set off on their worthy cause,
But when they came to look around, no solution could be found.
That cow was fast without a doubt, an' nowt on earth could get her out.
"There's only one thing left," they said,
" We'll have to saw off thow'd cow's 'yed".
So one and all they set to work, upon that poor unlucky stirk.

When their sorry task was o'er and t'cow lay stiff upon the floor,
A lad from Litton passing by, chanced to hear the last mournful cry,
And looking over the wall he found, the cow lying headless on the ground.
"Na' then! Whot's up 'ere?" he cried, at which the farmers all replied:
"She'd got 'er horns fast up 'ith gate, We've 'ad to cut 'er 'yed off mate!"

The Litton lad laughed out aloud, and said,
"Why 'an 'yer sawn off th'owd cow's yed?
It would a cost you less by far,
If instead yow'd sawn through t'bar!"

The Tidza chaps , they looked aghast,
They'd have to do some thinking fast
Ere they become the butt of all, from Castleton to Wormhill Hall.
So off they forced this Littonite, and did their best to get him tight.
They plied him with the strongest ales, a liquid he consumed in pails.
They persuaded him that what he'd seen,
Was a mirage on the village green.

Now if you think this story not quite true,
There's a Litton lad who'll swear to you,
That coming o'er Cliffe Lane one night, he'd had a very nasty fright.
And the cause of his alarm,
Was a cow-with it's head tucked 'neath it's arm!

Joe Chapman.

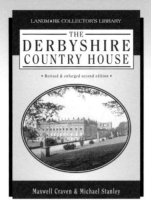
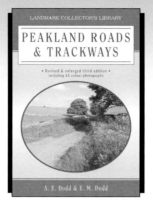

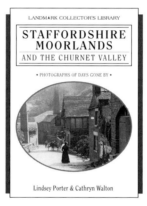
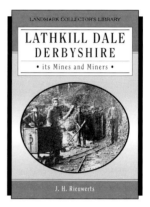
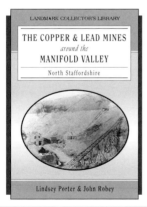
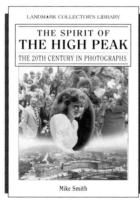
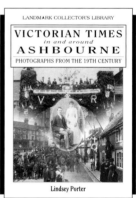